T0080028

Walking with
Ruskin

———

Walking with Ruskin

POEMS

Robert Cording

CavanKerry ◊ Press LTD.

Copyright © 2010 by Robert Cording
All rights reserved.

All rights reserved. No part of this book may be used, reproduced or
adapted to public performances in any manner whatsoever without
permission from the publisher, except in the case of brief quotations
embodied in critical articles and reviews. For more information, write
to Permissions, CavanKerry Press, 6 Horizon Rd., Ft. Lee, NJ 07024.

CavanKerry Press Ltd.
Fort Lee, New Jersey
www.cavankerrypress.org

Library of Congress Cataloging-in-Publication Data

Cording, Robert.
Walking with Ruskin : poems / by Robert Cording.
p. cm.
ISBN-13: 978-1-933880-21-1 (alk. paper)
ISBN-10: 1-933880-21-X (alk. paper)
I. Title.

PS3553.O6455W35 2010
811'.54--dc22

2010013639

Cover art Peggy MacNamara © 2010

Cover and interior design by Gregory Smith

First Edition 2010, Printed in the United States of America

NOTABLE VOICES
CavanKerry⊗Press

CavanKerry Press is proud to publish the works
of established poets of merit and distinction.

CavanKerry Press is grateful for the support it
receives from the New Jersey State Council on the Arts.

BOOKS BY
ROBERT CORDING

Poetry

Life—list (1987)

What Binds Us to This World (1991)

Heavy Grace (1996)

Against Consolation (2002)

Common Life (2006)

Edited

In My Life: Encounters with the Beatles (1998)
(eds: Cording, Jankowski-Smith, Miller-Laino)

Contents

Contents

III. Backward

IV. Here

V. A Map

Acknowledgements

Grateful acknowledgment is made to the following journals in which many of these poems were first published, sometimes in slightly different versions:

AGNI: April, Peepers, Flaubert and Springsteen; Mozart's Starling

Boston College Magazine: Room with Three Windows; Kin

Cave Wall: Cows

Chautauqua Literary Journal: Brother Woodpecker

Christianity and Literature: Dangling; Why I Live Here

Connecticut Review: Old Houses; Alligator Boy; Murmurings

Ecotone: In Early Spring

Georgia Review: Last Things; Walking with Ruskin

Harvard Review: Dandelions and Clover

Image: Erasure; Reading George Herbert; Four Prayers

Margie: At the Cemetery with Cotton Mather and Thomas Hardy

Ontario Review: January; Chances

Acknowledgments

Orion: Thirty Second Concert; Snake Crossing

Ploughshares: Gift

Post Road: Shame

Sewanee Review: Without End; Rain, Snow, Rain

Southern Review: The Chair; Sparrows; Luna Moths; Czeslaw Milosz's Glasses

Tri-Quarterly: Nocturne; On a Drop of Rain; Waiting for the Word

I'm also grateful to Judith Kitchen and Ted Kooser for including "Swallow Syllabics" in *The Poets Guide to the Birds,* Anhinga Press, 2009; to Philip Zaleski for including "Luna Moths" in *Best American Spiritual Writing,* 2007, and "Czeslaw Milosz's Glasses" in *Best American Spiritual Writing,* 2011; to Kurt Brown and Harold Schechter for including "On a Drop of Rain" in *Conversation Pieces,* Knopf, Everyman's Library, 2007.

For comments on earlier versions of these poems, I'm grateful to Bob Deppe, Brad Davis, Gray Jacobik, Baron Wormser and especially, William Wenthe and Jeffrey Harrison.

For Janet and Brian Avery
and in loving memory of their son, Brian

Every day the glory is ready to emerge from debasement.
—Rabbi Nachman of Bratslav

Movement is the best cure for melancholy.
—Robert Burton

Old Houses

Year after year after year
I have come to love slowly

how old houses hold themselves—

before November's drizzled rain
or the refreshing light of June—

as if they have all come to agree
that, in time, the days are no longer
a matter of suffering or rejoicing.

I have come to love
how they take on the color of rain or sun
as they go on keeping their vigil

without need of a sign, awaiting nothing

more than the birds that sing from the eaves,
the seizing cold that sounds the rafters.

I

All at Once

Dangling

When I believe I have no needs I cannot fulfill,
when my lies sound like truth,

and when I've added yet another self
to my fabrications, I contemplate the life of a monk

on Mt. Athos. It's said that he ties one end
of a rope to a cypress, then loops the other

around his chest and walks off the cliff where he lives.
Lord, you are my stronghold, he prays, dangling

a few hundred feet above the darker water
where the bottom drops off.

I suppose it's a way of restoring the grace
of insignificance, hanging like that

between the sky and the sea. I like to think
my thinking is a form of spiritual exercise,

but I never reach that moment
of unburdening when the monk feels at ease

(or so I wish), free now that he's tethered
again to God, when he needs nothing

that is not provided by the sea floating up on air,
its scent alone like the taste of the richest oysters.

No, for me, each day's fresh start points only
to the tree, the rope, the cliff-edge and sea.

And the going over, again and again.

Staying Awake

I've spent one third of my life asleep,
I read, and so I considered
how the drag and suck of Everyday
conspires against my waking—
jobs, meetings, grocery shopping,
house repairs and mortgages.

After I'd added on the dread of everything
I should have done but didn't, or did,
and had things turn out the very way
I'd feared, I just wanted to lie back
and dream, but I made myself sit up
in my chair, which brought to mind

my grandmother who liked to tell me
at family dinners, if I didn't sit up
straight, I'd become a hunch-back
as an old man, and now I was one,
at least in part, my shoulders slumping
forward, too heavy to hold up.

By then I was living in the past,
those dinners when all my grandparents
were alive, and my great-grandparents
on my mother's side and all my aunts
and uncles. I was saying their names—
Anna, Henry, Eleanor, Emma, George—

when, of course, I fell asleep and dreamed
that someone was whispering,
Wake up! Wake up! in a room
that the afternoon sun had warmed,
but now was running out of light.
And still I did not wake up.

Thirty Second Concert

(Orcas Island, Washington)

Just now,
overlapping,

the sound of water
against rock, against rock,

and, diminuendo,
with less *plock,* against driftwood,

and lower still, the ostinato
of a distant, invisible plane

playing in counterpoint
to a white-crowned sparrow's clear
first two alto notes

and the zigzag cacophony
of a kingisher's rattle—

here and gone—
passing into three caws
of a crow

as if every sound
connected to another,

or as if one sound
were making itself completely new
again and again,

even this deerfly's buzzing vibrato
one of the voices

that slide into or under
or over another,

and take place
all at once and at every moment,
though I hear it all

for no more
than thirty seconds
before the self's deafness returns.

Murmurings

As soon as I turned fifty he appeared.
He likes to look over my shoulder
when I falter over too many choices
of cereals at *Stop and Shop,* or drift through
my one hundred and twenty cable channels;
and he's beside me when I'm trying to decide
if I need more life insurance.

Last week, when I sat reading
by an open window, the lilacs outside
breathing into the room and filling it
with that sweet sensation of being
in just the right place, I thought I heard him
say, *you're always putting your bovine faith
in the pastures of what's comfortable.*

Ever since his arrival, I keep finding things
that need to be done, or done over—
a door that never swung right
on its hinges, mildew that's charting
a map again on the bathroom ceiling,
windows that need re-glazing,
a corner board rotting near a downspout.

Even the books I turn to for instruction
all seem to point to each other
rather than a direction I can follow.
And there he is, behind me, murmuring—
you know, every one of your thoughts

is really just a refuge where you believe
you can lie down and rest.

Lately, I believe my day of reckoning
has already come, and that my sentence
is this nagging companion
who likes to sneak up behind me
as I watch a pot of not yet boiling water,
and sneer: *I bet you'll die just like this, waiting*
for your life to break into rapture.

Czeslaw Milosz's Glasses

I.

Shortly after his death, they came to me
in a blue velvet Sailor fountain pen case,

a gift from a poet-friend who found Milosz
had left his glasses behind at a poetry festival.

By the time she reached him, he had
already bought a new pair. He's wearing

them in a photograph on the back cover
of *Second Space*; he's writing a poem,

or pretending to be for the photograph.
I like to think he's listening to the *daimonion*

he sometimes heard, writing down what it said—
faithfully. Yet he scoured every poem

for the disguises he knew were his, and unavoidable,
no matter how carefully he tried to listen.

II.

His glasses fit my wide head. I like to
put them on, but when I look through them,

the spruce tree outside my window is no longer
a spruce tree, hardly a tree at all; his glasses

make my head hurt. Which is meet and right,
as the Prayer Book says, no one knowing

better than him how the eyes are a temptation.
So much evil in believing that others see

the world just as we do. He knew words
could never navigate the roundness of things,

and yet knew, too, his work was to catch
the complexity of all in one unwritable sentence

he tried to write again and again.
Such a long journey to describe things

as they are. Sunlit depths of rivers. A wood
table set with plates for dinner. The roundness

of pears. The shape of a woman's breasts under
a summer dress. And also: a Nazi putting out

a cigarette on a Jewish child's arm. A pregnant
woman lying in a Warsaw street, being kicked,

begging for the blows to end. Families taken away,
wherever they were herded to, a nowhere.

III.

I met him once. He read his poems, and after
we had dinner with some others. I never said

how much I admired him, the poems.
We talked about the Psalms, their thirst for justice,

and he said man's instinctual sense of
what ought to be was precisely (and *perversely*,

he added) what lay behind the appeal
of propaganda in the modern era, lies

always more alluring and comforting
than reality. He drank too much and, rising

from the table with his cane, stumbled
and fell—something I tell only because

I feel he, who knew his faults better than anyone,
would have wanted me to. As he approached

his 90th year, he wrote that his former lives
were like *ships departing*, that the countries, cities

and gardens he'd known all this time, were "ready now
to be described better than they were before"—

as if he'd just received a new prescription,
and could see, at least for the time being,

more clearly through his newest glasses.
I keep his old glasses in my desk drawer,

and take them out at times when I begin
a poem. Not for inspiration, but for correction.

Reading George Herbert

All he ever wanted was to disappear.
But he kept coming upon himself
as if he were a character in a story
who, despite his best efforts to understand,
remained inscrutable. He tried
to keep straight the difference between
who the author said he was and who he
thought he was. He told himself again
and again that God was closer to him
than he was to himself. Still, he couldn't

close the distance. He was always getting
lost in his own plot, going off in all
the wrong directions. His own words
never helped, being always full of
a wild hunger, self-propulsive.
Prayer helped. But even when he heard
a melody not his own, when he'd try
to sing it, what came out of him
was off-key and horribly out of tune.

Each day he went to war against himself,
but he could never disarm himself.
Yet, waking, he'd often relish the new day,
tasting the sweetness of the world
he accepted as an undeserved gift.
And, in its clear and shimmering air,
he'd sometimes see a road that ran straight
to the open door of paradise,
though the moment he started walking,

the day would be diminished by the weight
of clouds that gradually lugged themselves
all the way to the horizon. How could he
not help but think, *sure, of course,*
just as I expected, just what I deserved?
Once, having travelled farther
from himself than he'd ever been,
he believed he heard God saying, *Yes, this way*
come ahead, enter, but he was only human,
and thought the voice must be his own.

Waiting for the Word

A right arm she can't lift up, a left hand
that's still no good at managing a fork;
the mild summer weather she remembers
from childhood and the crazy, overheated
weather these days; the once upon a time
that is never enough; and the dead
still demanding to be remembered
by a mind steadily failing; the mourning
doves that don't know a damn thing
about sadness, and a God always taking
back what he gives—and then, *Nevertheless*
arrives as always, her phone soliloquy
continuing with the chickadees outside
her window, the smell of pine trees after rain,
the pretty pink and gray-ribbed undersides
of the squatting clouds, a towhee insisting
she drink her tea, and the sunny, less humid
days due sometime at the week's end.

The Chair

There's a chair in the snow-covered field
where I left it, and you, dead now a year,
are sitting in it, looking at three crows,
their black nearly burning in the morning
sun. *Thanks for the chair,* you say, when I
make some crack about where will the dead
turn up next, unsurprised by your being
here. I left it just for you, I say, and maybe
I did. And maybe you're here because
I cannot stop loving you, and maybe this
is all a dream, but I don't want to wake up
before you answer all those questions I have—
not so much about the afterlife, but about
the unfairness of things here, in particular
who suffers and why, and maybe something
about God's silence—but already you've put
your fingers to your lips, still looking at the crows,
at home in the cold, a little cape of snow
warming you. I keep chattering away
about the shitty state of the world, listing
my complaints as if you were a messenger
between my world and the next.
But snow is falling through me, as if I
were suddenly porous and every boundary
had been removed, and I am shining
in the light it makes. When I look to you,
you are gone and I have not said how much
I've missed you, nor how, at times, I've prayed

to you. And whatever peace you brought
is interrupted now by my fears—how dwarfed I am
by the field and the sky filling the empty chair
with snow. Then my waking sense
of everything missed, and missing again.

On a Drop of Rain

Late in the day, the rain abating,
I force myself outside for my daily walk.
I do not go far. Everything is doused
and diamonded with water. Even the stones
seem polished. At each bud of every scrub
roadside tree, and even on the thorns
of wild roses, hangs a drop of rain—
as if someone had hoisted chandeliers
to light the road from end to end.

I think of Marvell, how he found a story
one morning shining with meaning
in a drop of dew. A figure for the soul,
Marvell's dewdrop contained the whole
sky and, mindful of its native home,
came and went, scarcely touching
the earthly flower on which it floated,
its one aspiration the sunny exhalation
of water into air. It never seemed to feel

death's shiver. Here, it's nearly evening,
the air still rheumy enough to silver
the weedy edge of the road where beer cans
find their rest. My raindrops—tense, trembling—
really do seem to cling for dear life,
a story, I'm sad to say, of my all too earthly
wish to hang around forever in my body.
No chance, the wind says, extinguishing
with every breeze, one drop after another.

Erasure

It's what I need to practice,
the lines of my life too neatly drawn
around the comfort of being here.

It's why I'm out here again,
in the middle of the field just as
the day pauses between what is

and what was, darkness rising up
between the hemlocks and spruces
that have brought their shadows

together. I'm waiting for the moment
when the oaks and ashes
slip out of the names we gave them,

the thrushes have had their say
and the dark adds the slightest chill
to the air, a breeze announcing itself

in the wind-chimes. It's then
that the invisible hearse of darkness
waits for me to get in. It's then

that I too often call out, *here*
I am, to someone who has just begun
to wonder where I have gone.

II

In and Out

Chances

Chances are . . . I remember
a state policeman beginning. I don't remember
the odds, only how much depended

on what lay beyond our control,
a Hasidic girl from Brooklyn missing, lost
during a school trip

in our local northeast Connecticut woods.
Volunteers, we were told she was wearing
a long blue skirt, a windbreaker
that might keep her warm—

if she was still alive,
I couldn't keep from thinking.

Spring was cold and wet that year
and a rainstorm was taking shape
as the first day darkened.

I thought of her parents more than the girl.
That question they must have asked of themselves:
What can we do to do something?

How could they keep from picturing the terror
that could be happening, even then, to her?

Could they be sure they had loved her enough?

———————

On the second day: six hundred Hasidim
arrived from New York, Boston, Montreal.
Helicopters blew over the tops of pines.

In the woods, one thousand volunteers
called the girl's name as if we were calling
our own child to come in.

How could she be lost? her parents kept asking.

They'd watched their child
wave to them from a bus window
just the day before.

Now her Xeroxed face was taped
in every restaurant window.

Whenever the sun broke through,
we said, with forced conviction,
that chances were good we'd find her.

I kept seeing the girl,
then, in my mind, my own children,
as if part of me was looking for
the small child they had been,

still mine, still protected,
not already wandering in the half-tragic,
half-comic teenage years

of discovering how anything can happen,
but rarely in the way they had wanted.

Everywhere, walls of rhododendrons,
thickets of wirey brush. No footprints in the mud,

my own feet mired with the weight
of what I had always known
but mostly could forget: that some horror

is happening somewhere every minute of the day.

On the third day, a light rain.
We affected the expression of good cheer.

Someone was always calling on Hope,
someone was always shaking their head
and saying, our chances were running out.

And then, under an ash tree, the shadow of a girl
slowly becoming the girl in the blue skirt,
as if, this time, the woods were giving her back.

Cold, frightened, okay, she waved
as if she had been expecting us all this time.

She let us lift her, exhausted.

That night on the local stations:
the girl coming out of the woods over and over,

ringed by Hasidim dancing and singing,
nothing held in reserve for a better day.

And her parents, draped over her, sobbing,
their joy complicated with the intricacies of fear.

I remember how I wiped the tears
from my eyes, then moved towards my car,
as if I could simply go home now

to my family—which I did, still stunned
by my hunger for light, my instinctive knowledge

of the dark; by what did not happen
and what did, all efforts ending in those
two possible chances.

Shame

Four last night. They trickled into the church
before the cold solidified. My wife and I signed them in,
made them empty pockets, checked for drugs and weapons,
went over the copious medications they carried,
then let them graze on free coffee, oranges, bread,
crackers, peanut butter, even a large bag
of Kentucky Fried wings a parishioner
brought by—gifts and leftovers of our middle class.

Once a month or so in the winter, my wife and I
volunteer to open the doors and sleep on the floor
with whoever needs to come in out of the cold,
mostly castaways of the state that cuts costs
by closing down the mental hospitals. Again,
the shock of fitting their lives into ours:
how normal everyone appeared at first, and then,
inexorably, their oddnesses leaked out.

Karen—articulate, well-educated—talked about
Exodus, then waved her hand suddenly to reveal five
angels that help her communicate with her children,
taken away years back: *trouble with the Feds* over her politics.
Off in the corner, Ed, who had a pocketful of meds, said
he'd married a deaf and dumb woman who played around.
When he hit her, hard, she moved to Florida.
Ed never sleeps, afraid he'll dream of her, whom he *loves*

more than my life. Jim—alcoholic, depressed, unstable—
is trying to get to Florida (their crazy bond) where his father

is dying, but he doesn't know what town. And Deanna?
She came just to help out, she said, though it's clear
this group is her only family. And then what needed to be told
was told, and what could not be told moved back into
the confusion of their minds. As if they'd just remembered
no one would tell them, "It will be all right, all right,"

everyone went utterly quiet, retreating to what they do
by rote—gather blankets, wash, pee, divide themselves
into the rooms for women and men. So we slept,
heat at the center, the oil burner droning out the dream talk,
the groaning and shifting of weight. Near dawn, I saw Ed
sitting up, then leaning back on his arms as if he were caught
in a contradiction he couldn't resolve, waiting for
the morning, and wishing it would never come.

It came, the sun a disc of white in the steel-colored sky.
My wife and I locked the church, and warmed up our car.
Our group of night visitors bunched up against the wall.
They could have been the brunt of God's joke
about the last who shall be first. No biblical edge
of the field left to glean, for them it's store-front
encampments, and the shuffling in and out of the cold
according to the good will and shame of the owners.

Sparrows

A certain traveler who knew many continents
was asked what he found most remarkable
of all. He replied: the ubiquity of sparrows.

—Adam Zagajewski, *Another Beauty*

Sparrow: our generic for any of the small brown birds
we find everywhere. A farm field in early April,
nothing yet green. Or a sidewalk downtown

edged with February's dirty snow, a scrap
of paper with someone's name on it
skittering in a gust of building-tunneled wind.

Sparrows: fussing about in the dirt, washing
themselves in a gutter's runoff, hanging on
the dry seed head of a winter weed.

Barn, strip mall, field, swamp, college ivy,
Walmart sign: all places to prove their gift for
survival. Like the poor, they are their own keepers.

Once in Palestine there were so many, two
could be had for the price of one farthing,
but Jesus said his father knew each one of them,

just as the hairs on our head were numbered.
Those must have been house sparrows; they were
fruitful and multiplied because they fed on

the droppings of horses and cattle. Sparrows.
I never learned them well enough. They slipped
in and out of my focus, the color of dust

and dirt, common-featured. *Field sparrow,*
fox sparrow, song sparrow, swamp sparrow.
It took so much attention to give a name

to them, the way, too often, I see the poor
only as that, their faces hidden as they lie
like sacks on grates of vented heat. Ubiquitous.

Common-featured. How can they be seen
when they are always in sight? When Jesus
laid his hands on the faces of the poor,

I'd like to believe he saw them as they wanted
to be seen: each a child who belonged
to somebody, who once had a given name.

On the Way to Cold Mountain

An hour ago, wind cleaned up
the remaining stale air
a cold front had pushed away,
and the morning was sunshine
and breeze. I was singing
Simon and Garfunkel,
and slowing down, making
the morning last, grinning
like an idiot, crazy with
the wild exchange of sunlight
and green leaves taking place
in the lilac. The sweet scent
of Rambling Roses preceded
the thought of roses, and you
came to mind, Han Shan,
saying, *Be happy, if there's
something to be happy about.*
And there was. I was happy
about the day and, going inside,
the beautiful old room I sat in
and the black tea with milk
I drank. I should have put up
a sign—*No Philosophizing Today*—
and just lain down on the rug
like my dog turning once, twice,
and then curling in on herself.

You also said, *when the moment
comes, do not lose it*—but I did,

a neighbor coming to mind
who hears voices that speak
inside his head. And then, all
those who walk in madness
in every city, and of how, if I
were asked by any one of them
to give up my life for theirs,
I could not. Who could?—
O Han Shan, it's right and true
that happiness doesn't need
to be deserved and, believe me,
I exult over birdsong, I'm
grateful for the clearing rain
and storm-freshened air,
the great banquet of light
at my window. But tell me,
is there some small measure
of happiness for those
who can never lose themselves
in these moments—
so excessive and splendid—
that rush toward us, and away?

Alligator Boy
(Costa Rica)

I just wanted to see some new birds—
green parrots, scarlet macaws, maybe a trogon—
but my guide, just fourteen that very day,
could not believe birds were enough.

So as darkness lifted up from the river,
the boy pulled his boat on shore
and slipped himself into the brown water,
carrying a sack he'd loaded earlier.

Up to his waist, his small, muscled chest
hardening in the cooling air,
he removed two freshly killed chickens
and began to clap them together,

the beat and scent of them drawing
an alligator from the opposite shore.
He wanted me to take pictures. He wanted
to be seen. I watched, fascinated, fearful,

part of a plot I had not bargained for
and could not redirect, my hands shaking
as the alligator closed the distance
between them, its serpentine tail twitching

steadily back and forth. Thirty feet away,
the alligator slipped underwater and the boy,
too, lowered himself beneath the surface.
When they came up, no more than ten feet

from each other, the boy held out
the chickens in his outstretched hand
and waited, his gaze so focused he seemed
to be receiving millions of impressions

from the last light that barely touched
the moving surface of the water. And then,
as if from the start there never had been
any choice but this very end, the alligator

reared up, its prehistoric jaws opening
and snapping shut on the chickens.
The boy smiled, held up his empty hands.
I took his picture—his arms upraised

as if in victory. I have it still, though I sent
him all the others. In it, he's proved
himself, proved he could earn the money
I paid him and he held in his hand

all the way home to those crimped,
roadside, dirt-floored, tin-scrabbled houses
where I dropped him off, and tried hard
not to look at what he did not want me to see.

Snake Crossing

But not even a sign could save you.
When one of your kind tries to cross
the road—no matter how close, it seems,
you are to one side or the other—
some car seems bound to make straight
your sinewy motion, and someone,
I imagine, looks back
over his or her shoulder, as satisfied
to have gotten you as they might be
to cross some task off their to-do list,
or to fix that one thing they believed
was always wrong with their lives.

Rain, Snow, Rain

Without plot,
the day out-

side my window
slips from snow

to rain, slips
from little drips

of water to silence—
the rain's presence

within the snow,
and again the snow.

Inside I can't sort
the sordid facts

of a neighbor's
unthinkable murder

in this rural town
of five thousand.

Rain, snow, rain,
and, within,

without relief,
anger and grief

looking out
on an inky net

of winter branches—
my exposed nerves

will not be
calmed by the easy

passage of water
from hour to hour,

so much welling up
I cannot stop,

so much that outruns
the mind's stubborn

need to make sense
where no sense is.

III

Backward

January

This month's god faced backward and forward,
as you do, your son dead one month.

Blind to the present, you live between
a past already bleeding away and a future

no longer coming, but here. You wear
his shirts, sit among gathered photographs

of life together before the accident. To move on,
you repeat to yourself, *what is taken is first a gift,*

but you keep subtracting his thirteen years
from a lifespan you once believed was given.

One year has ended, another begun; the light lost,
is now returning— what good does it do to say

these things, you ask, when the hours pass,
but not the wound that keeps remembering.

You hope for dreams in which your dead son
greets you, but when you lie down your mind wakes

to what has already been. You close your eyes.
You open your eyes. The white air of January presses

up against the bedroom window. You look
down and up the street. Snow has fallen,

and someone about your son's size
is walking a dog toward the lake. You wish

he would turn his head and look back
in your direction. You lean forward,

until your forehead touches the cold glass.

Four Prayers

I. March Prayer

What do I do to keep the image of her
bent over her dead son as alive as this bluebird—
elegant and simple, and perfectly made for delight—
releasing its blue to the sky? How do I speak
of a mother bent over her son's body
as if he could still recognize it was she there
alongside him, ready to go wherever he was going . . .
and also of this morning that arrived fresh and new,
old piles of snow being eaten by a March sun,
water running everywhere, the *hey sweetie* of chickadees
leafing the leafless trees. O Lord, this is
what I know: grief is endless, delight unavoidable.
Teach me to live in this contradiction, help me
to keep seeing her desiccated mouth, the sorrow
in her throat she could not swallow, her eyes
that still, months later, cannot see
this bluebird which I cannot enjoy any less.

II. *June Prayer*

Pray for me, she said, and Lord I try.
I have no eye for eternity. I know
only this world, where May's light lengthens
into June's long days, and someone I love
keeps discovering that grief is a season
that leads nowhere. Lord, take pity

45

on this prayer which is meant to be plain,
to ask no more than what has always been
asked—that she be helped to bear the weight
she cannot bear alone. But I cannot refrain
from asking something more: Why,
if she can still perfectly recall the horror
she most wants to forget, why, as the months
pass, is she already losing the feel of her son's
touch and the exact timbre of his voice
when he joked with her? Lord, the sun is
stronger each day and the trees have filled
with birds again, but all she sees
are the boys she must forgive each day
for living, for bouncing a basketball or
carrying their mitts and bats. And she does.
She does. Can you not, then, help her lift
her head and say again—*Blessed is the day*—
words, perhaps, that might release her
from her season of captivity in the dark
belly of memory where she waits for you.

III. *October Prayer*

It rains, it rains, and the leaves, more brown
than gold, come off like a child's soaked
clothes. One season collapses
into another. For ten months, Lord,
I have gone down to the place where the dead
are shut away. I have wanted to speak
with the authority of *It came to pass,*

or *verily I say to you* to one I dearly love,
but I have no powers to restore the blood
that drained from the veins of her child.
Only, *this must be endured,* as if endurance
could lighten the weight of her grief.
She keeps measuring her grief against
the grief of others—one thirteen year old
against the thirty million children dead
each year, one son against the thousands
lost to starvation, to war, just one against
the tens of thousands lost in an earthquake.
Each day, she counts the losses; today,
a father's three young children and his wife
to a mudslide that buried their home.
Why is it, she wants to know, that one
lost son can so empty the entire world?
Why, she asks, can't she *move forward,*
find the strength, rise to the occasion,
get through it? Lord, she knows too well
she is not the center of anything,
and yet she remains, waiting still
at the place where her son left her, waiting
for the spirit said to ease us. I have
waited for a prayer, for some words to help
her believe what can never be changed can be
endured and made easier in its suffering
as I walked in circles in these wet woods,
the leaves down, here and there another
fresh stump where a tree has fallen over
staring upwards, the lines of trees against
one another like a child's scribblings
that do not mean a thing.

IV. *December Prayer*

For seven days the sword is drawn,
for thirty days it wavers; and after
twelve months, it returns to its scabbard—
the wisdom of the Talmud, a recognition
of death's hold on the living
left behind. Lord, her year is done
and, if nothing else, your silence
has taught her daily that her son
must be given up sense by sense,
thought by thought, action by action.
Just a year and a day ago
he would have made her laugh
or argued with her or talked back.
Now December is dying once again
into the roosting dark: cold air, cold
flame, the sky burning itself clean.
Lord I ask this much for her,
who knows too well she will go on
missing him until she dies: let rooms
made small by the violence of grief
be amplified by the wan light
the sun hoists up over the inch
of new winter snow. Let there be
laughter again at the kitchen table,
let the spoons and forks make a racket
on the plates, and the youngest's
spilled glasses of milk be seen
as cups running over. Let her eyes,
blinded for so long by grief, see again
what is just outside her window:

a red and white clownish woodpecker,
two nuthatches spiraling head first
down a tree, the neighbor in her
nightgown who holds out her hands
with five different kinds of seed,
a suburban St. Francis of the birds,
and another, like Moses, waving
and honking in clouds of white exhaust
as he backs out of his driveway and leads
a string of cars toward the station.
Lord, give her this day. For one year
she has waited out the empty rehearsals
of hope. And she will go on living with
the pain of what will never make sense.
But Lord, death's year is up. Let the sun
pass over her face as she sits by the window.
When the early dark arrives, let her watch
the sky orchestrate the last orange glints
the day becomes. Let that be an end of it . . .

Without End

Because she gave him life, she must bury
her dead child inside herself,
a labor without end, but one she undertakes.
Because she gave him life once,
she must do so again, one cell at a time if necessary:

limb buds, pits where his blue eyes will be,
caverns and ridges to reveal a brain
and heart, his neck and face;
and after, those first signs of wrists and ankles,
his five webbed fingers and toes.

Her child will not toss or turn or kick for more
space as he once did. He will not be reborn.
She knows this. But because she gave him life,
her child must be carried with her—there is no other way—
for the full term of her remaining life.

Kin

If the work of grieving is to remain
grief-stricken, and if grief's absence
is worse than its pain, then she has no choice
but the one she chooses—to let the weight
of her dead child grow heavier, to let it
crush the spring's new leaves and grasses,
the magnolia's and cherry's flowering.

And if, despite all our prayers to *Help her,
O Lord, to lay down her burdens,* she lifts up
her bundle of sadness and sorrow each day,
then let her be comforted by its weight
and the task of carrying it; and if one day,
nearly a year after her son has died,
there's another occasion for bells,

though this time they chime for a wedding,
and the day, though rain was predicted,
has opened out into yellow and green dresses
winking in the sun and a whirling breeze
that blows open the blues and whites
of suits and shirts and makes kites of ties,
then let the day be joyous even for her.

And if, finally, the ritual complete,
she's gathered among sisters and brothers
and someone tells a joke, then let there be
praise for that which achingly begins
somewhere deep inside her and spreads

like hunger until it must be fed, and she
laughs for the first time, quietly, then louder.

And even if she feels horrified now,
her laughter uncontrollable, ravenous,
let there be wonder for the way its grip
is briefly stronger than the grip of death,
as if some god, seeing the hold of grief,
said, *Let there be lively quivers of laughter,*
kin to grief's ululation of heaving sobs.

IV

Here

Stopping By the Pond

I've come a snowy mile
with nothing in mind,
it now seems, but to stand
at the eastern end
of this iced-over pond,
looking at the afternoon's
quiet subtractions—
white the road, and white
the hills that rim the pond,
and white my breath
that's blown across the pond.

Brim-full with snow
that's wind-raked
and whorled evenly,
the pond, in my seeing,
becomes a Zen garden.
A dark green ladder
of shoreline white pines
acts as counterpoint;
Even the stumps of trees
at the pond's far end
seem carefully arranged

to stretch the pond
toward the pale gray infinite
horizon of taut sky
where a plane is rising
gradually out of Hartford,

leaving me (who
would be no more
from the plane's vantage
than a well-placed stone),
to walk out of my garden
and trudge the mile home.

In Early Spring

The fields were still matted,
and dirty snow huddled
in patches, but the swing
of the earth had taken place

and it tilted toward the sun's
warmth that heated up
the back of my neck.
When I passed the horse

I pass every day on my walk,
it whinnied and tossed
its head back and forth—
perhaps a touch of sun

worship in him
or the need to shake off
months of cold, or maybe
to shake me from myself—

and for once it had
my undivided attention,
and it bent its long neck down
to a ball and ran, its head

moving the ball left then
right with the deft touch
of a soccer player. Again
and again, it cut and drove

the ball from one end
of its ring to the other,
Spring's energy moving
through its body, flanks

and hooves taking form,
its tail and mane becoming
the single unbroken line
of a prehistoric horse

drawn on the muscled stone
of a cave wall. Standing there,
the soft animal of my body
roused itself, and I began to run—

not far and downhill mostly—
toward the pond where, bent over,
chest heaving, I stopped
to laugh at myself and catch

my breath. Six geese
skidded in, a towhee
and then a redwing blackbird
called out, and the light

on the water quickened
in a breeze, each thing
shaping itself to the shape
of the minute, the month,

the season, the turning earth.

Why I Live Here

Because the view is always partial,
small-paned, the sky parceled out by trees.

Because I like the grey and brown birds
and how they flit in and out of my vision

in the grey and brown woods,
endless versions of what can and cannot be seen.

And because I like the mystery of an old truck
that suddenly appears in the middle

of these roadless, second-growth woods,
a maple sapling growing from the windshield,

its backseat a storehouse for nuts,
a chickadee bathing on its caved-in roof.

Or how my eyes can map winter's bare-limbed roll
of hills, each lost, then found again as I walk.

Because I can sit in the woods and watch
a white-tailed deer move from one leg

to another, never once putting a foot
completely down, always ready to disappear.

Sitting there, I've noticed the brotherhood
of mosses on trees and stones,

and the intricate, beetled life of dead trees.
Still, there's always something I never quite see—

a vole (?) moving under leaves, or a grouse (I think)
that's only tail feathers disappearing into a thicket

of spirea. Where I live is good practice
at reading from the Book of Concealments.

Because the ancient stories have already said
how we can travel to the gods and back,

or emerge from the labyrinthine underworld
and still not know enough, I'm preparing

for the last page when the story some expect
to be revealed in full still surpasses understanding.

My Neighbor's Mailbox

The first time some teens, buzzed on beer
or coke, caved in her mailbox with a bat,
a new one appeared the very next day,

but with two small hand-painted geese
on the routine black metal where the flag
is raised. When that one was crushed,

her next gave both sides to a scene
of woods and field and a small brook
that joined each other at the door.

After yet a third time the mailbox
and even the post was taken out, she built
a little red barn out of wood

with a door that opened to receive
the mail. Below the mailbox, she placed
a flower pot, of deep blue porcelain,

filled with salmon-colored lilies . . .
Often I see her pulling weeds, watering
the open-throated lilies, tending to

the spot of ground around the mailbox
as if Martin Buber were right, and God allots
to each of us our own little area to redeem.

Of course her actions may only prove again
how thin the line between divinity and madness.
Or that she may be merely holding on

to some principle learned in Sunday school,
those kids no more to her than a test
of neighborly love. But maybe

she sees those boys, whoever they are,
with girlfriends and high school classes,
all of them rushing into what lies ahead

without a sense yet of who they might be;
and maybe she can imagine them
arriving one night only to pull back their bat

and just laugh, the barn door open,
a letter lying like a beast in its stall, the night air
disarming, charged with the scent of lilies.

Walking with Ruskin

Each day I walk for an hour or two,
what started as exercise now a matter
of devotion. Or, less grandly:
walking gives me something to do,
a kind of discipline since I don't know
how to move towards any of those
big intangible goals—wholeness, God,
forgiveness, justice—but I know how
to walk. Sometimes I bring Ruskin along.

Despite his holy striving and cloying
superlatives ("the greatest thing
a human soul does in the world is
to see something," or "art springs from
the most profound admiration"),
I like the way he forgets himself
in his concern for what is particular
about an eagle's beak or the green-brown
coppery iridescence of a pheasant's feather.

He's teaching me a kind of readiness
for what comes along as it pleases:
a line of ants carrying the remains
of a red emerald butterfly, or
a brook in winter moving under ice
like the one-celled life found in a drop
of water under a microscope.
I like to compare notes with him,
to count the shades of blue

on a kingfisher's back or the three
different kinds of wing feathers,
but I'm still learning to look at things
with Ruskin's respect for fact
and his love for what's being seen—
this beetle, say, that's crossed our path,
its two topside eyes ringed in white,
the lacquer of its shell a depth
of black and darkest greens.

Today, the late July pond water looks
like used car oil, and the roadside grass
is a pointillist study of greens
and the bright white coffee cups of
Americans who run on Dunkin'.
Ruskin and I are looking at clouds,
a kind of medicine. Ruskin says,
they *calm and purify,* if only because
the sky is large and we are not.

And if I'm always half-thinking of
my credit card debt, or if I'm seven
to ten years of mortgaged life
away from retirement, I go on
crouching down for a beetle
that doesn't care if it's seen, though
my seeing it makes the day more real
to me. Nothing much, but something
I'm always thanking Ruskin for.

Swallow Syllabics

I walk where I always walk
  and as always each day
for a month now some forty swallows
  constantly re-arrange
themselves on the five lines that run from

pole to pole and span the field
  that's just been second-cut.
Seven on the top wire, six and nine
  on the two lines below,
and—count them—five, six, but already

they are flying off their lines,
  these scattering swallows
that almost enact the prosody
  I'd like to find by chance,
and would, perhaps, if my direction

towards them hadn't forced them
  into air. Seems they've got
my number, these swallows that sit in
  iconic disregard
until I approach and then, like sprung

syllables, take to the sky,
  perpetual motion,
their quick swerves and glides continuous,
  undoing any thought
that they could be settled onto lines.

At the Cemetery with Cotton Mather and Thomas Hardy

It's yet another day
of unrepentant rain,
of woods lush with rot
and streets streaked
with the remains of two turtles,
a squirrel's final unhousing
by a host of flies,
and a snake being picked over
by a crow whose appetite
for death will make clean work
of what's left by the time
I return this way tomorrow.

I'm more than half way along
my daily walk when I lean
against a cemetery tree
and empty myself
next to my squatting dog,
and think of Cotton Mather
peeing beside his dog—
of how he felt ashamed
of his animal nature,
and promised then and there
to let his higher spirit
rise and soar. As for mine,

it slaps at a horsefly
orbiting my head

and watches my salts disappear
in the grass. I guess
I'm more a fan of Hardy,
who once gave the names
of his beloved dead to the leaves
of a cemetery yew. For now
at least, my dog and I
going on our way, I think,
wouldn't it be fine
if a loved one of mine
saw me rising someday
in this sugar maple's leaves
whose roots I've just watered?

Dandelions and Clover

For weeks now, watching a groundhog
in my backyard, I've entertained the thought,
why not found a new nation, usher in
the Republic of the Groundhog? Why not
sew up a flag and put on it this sleepy monitor
of sunlight, dandelion greens, and clover?

Quaker-souled, the groundhog quickly retreats
to his hole if I close the door too loudly.
He knows the purity of giving in. I love
his easy-going slouch, the way he takes
the hurry out of living, teaching me to enjoy
these unearthly earthly times that invite us

to linger in June's salad days of green grass
and sun. A Stoic with the droll humor
of a Jewish comedian, he lives free
of illusion, close to the earth, and does not
worry about gaining weight or looking good,
his grizzled fur never once in vogue.

And when his time in the sun is up,
he is more than willing to wait in the dark,
bearing witness to everything in its proper time.
I bless this true believer in deliverance
who simply ignores the wishful adulation
of the ones who would declare his return,

dragging their hopes behind him like a shadow.
Seeing how he never needs more than he has,
and is so completely egoless he doesn't mind
being called by two different names,
I declare today the Republic of the Groundhog.
Or Woodchuck—take your pick.

Necessary Fool

She was what she was—a golden,
with a golden's therapeutic capacity
to please, always drooling love,
at any moment ready to roll over basely,
legs up in the air when I'd lean down to pet her.
A dog with an empty thought balloon
above a head tilted into the air, all attention
concentrated in her nose.

On walks, one of us was always trying
to work out the day's poem or compose tomorrow's
lecture; and one of us always close-reading
turds and peed-upon twigs and grass,
stopping now and again for what
seemed like nothing at all.
And sometimes I'd see it, a deer
mid-woods or a grouse I'd nearly stepped on.

A hermeneutist of dead leaves,
sometimes she'd lift up a vole and hold it
in her soft mouth as if to say,
the world's alive all around you.
I suppose it's just another bauble of imagination
that wants to see a dog (who, by her very nature
could not help but show me things
I could not see myself) as a kind of necessary fool

to my kingly self-absorption, but sometimes,
Nellie chewing grass she was destined to throw-up,
then lying down, the two of us pausing
on the hillside above the pond,
goldfinches flashing, a mallard floating by,
there'd come a moment when I'd grow
as thoughtless as my dog, my guide
it now seems, to something like a paradise.

V

Map

Cows

Today, three cows casually lifted up their heads
to me as I walked by, and time, undone for once,
returned one of the first mornings with our first child,
twenty-five years in the past. The three of us
were together in the bedroom of the rented house
in Ireland, as if we had never left that place
where our lives as parents first began.
And you and I were slowly waking to the sound
of a neighbor's cow as it licked the night's condensation
from our window which, gradually clearing,
allowed the day outside to come into being, the pale
blue light turning bluer. Out of fear the baby
would wake, we muffled our laughter over the way
that cow's massive head so comically filled the window,
its ears flicking non-stop, its huge wet eyes
delicately outlined by such oddly human lashes.
You joked that the cow had Buddha eyes—
I think you meant that strangely comforting pathos
of one who's seen everything and still accepts.
Or maybe that is just a way of saying how I felt
a calm settle over us. And while I would never wish
for perfect memory, its cost too much
pain brought back too precisely, I'm glad
this forgotten and unbidden moment was provided
by three cows I'd almost passed without notice, if only
because it gives me a second chance for proper gratitude.

Brother Woodpecker

(for our twenty-fifth wedding anniversary)

There is nothing that doesn't belong with love
—Gerald Stern

For two weeks, I took it the wrong way—
those holes in our shingles, the incessant knocking
that drove me from my desk
to lead yet another assault on the woodpecker
that flew casually to a nearby tree,
and turned his back on me.

Remember how I checked for insects,
bandaged our house with tin, and hammered back
a few loose shingles? Well, today,
just when I thought I couldn't take it anymore,
the woodpecker making a telegraph of the family room,
I got out Sibley's *Guide to Bird Behavior*.

And there it was, the help I'd been looking for,
the woodpecker's tock-tock-tock-tock
not mockery, but need: our house, for better
or worse, just a makeshift hollow tree,
his raucous drumming no more or less
than the declarations of mating.

Hell, if he were human, we'd call it love.
So knock yourself out, brother woodpecker,
and let's listen, dear, at least for now,

with new ears to the way its hard staccatos
are like those first wild beats we heard
so surely, and followed into this shared life.

It's That Time of Year

when everyone is taking off their clothes
on this first day of sunny seventy-five degrees
of Zen-weather, airing out, answering some instinct
for rapture that's been mothballed for months.
I'm talking in earnest about Milton,
but my class has long stopped listening to me.

Windows thrown open, my students
have become verbs, and the object they're seeking is
sitting right next to them, the jubilations of bare skin
like a paradise they've walked back into.
They just want to be happy as dogs rolling in the grass,
which is where they're headed as class ends.

How electric and irreversible
is the steady flow of energy right out the door! –
my students' idea of truth inseparable from the body
sprawled in the sun, hot to be part of the carnival
of every whistling bird, every seed-dropping flower
and tree, every fattening blade of grass.

"Find thyself a teacher," the Talmud says,
and today I choose my students
who have to be nowhere else but here,
each of them the center of one another's attention,
citizens in a democracy that truly welcomes
the pursuit of life, liberty, and happiness.

So praise be to flip-flops, to discarded shirts
lying like drunks in the grass;
to amped up dorms cranking out the healing touch
of Marley and the slow hand of Clapton;
and praise to these hours in which the solidarity
of the flesh defeats the worm of worry;

and to my teachers, relaxed masters, without thought
of past or future, who know how to welcome
this moment of pumped-up Chaucerian sparrows
singing their heads off from the ivy-covered
garden of a classroom building as they gather
their many separate desires into one flock.

April, Peepers, Flaubert, and Springsteen

Now that the sun's hanging around longer,
these first warm evenings bring
the peepers up out of the muck, aroused
by temperatures and a ferocious desire
to peep and trill a hundred times a minute,
nearly six thousand times a night,
each wet, shining body a muscle of need
that says *faster, louder, faster, louder.*

*Life, life, to have erections, that's what it's
all about*—that's Flaubert ringing
in my old ears, some drained chamber
of the heart pumping again, interrupting
my bookish evening. I should tie myself
to my chair or stopper my ears. But I'm up
and answering my sirens' call, overcome
by some need to be outside, to be
part of this great spring upheaval.

In the dark amid their chorus, I hold
a flashlight on a peeper that pulses
under its skin, its entire body a trill reaching
toward a silent female, and now I'm calling
to my wife to come out, to hurry,
and when she finds me, I swear I feel as if
I'm shining like something that has come up
from deep under the earth, and singing

It ain't no sin to be glad you're alive.

Nocturne

First wind, then rain, then sweetness
of air after rain, the sound of leaves emptying
in a fresh breeze. Then clouds loosening their grip
and stars sliding out from beneath. And trees,
shadows, deer, raccoon—stretching and
spreading out, taking on the night's nomadic lightness.

Only my dogged mind still fitting the day together
before sleep, Manichean in its desire to arrange
tomorrow into segments of morning and afternoon
sized to its needs, afraid to pray that one prayer
that might let it find rest: *O my little self,*
let the world stream by and be large.

Mozart's Starling

A little fool lies here
Whom I hold dear—
—Mozart, lines of a poem for his pet starling

None of his friends understood.
A poem for a bird?—
and a funeral, and the ridiculous
request that they dress in formal attire.

But when Mozart whistled a yet-to-be
fragment of a piano concerto
in the marketplace, the bird
may have sang it back to him—

the starling appears in his diary
of expenses, May 27, 1784,
along with a transcription of its song.
What fun they must have had,

he whistling a melody, the bird,
a virtuoso mimic, echoing it back,
interspersed among its clicks
and slurs and high-pitched squeals.

Music to Mozart's ears,
that dear bird who sang incessantly
for the duration of its three
short years in Mozart's company.

His *little fool* was wise indeed—
it could hear a squeaking door,
a teapot letting off its steam,
a woman crying or rain pinging

in metal buckets and gurgling
in gutters, even a horse's snort
or Mozart scratching notes,
and sing it back until Mozart, too,

could hear the cockeyed,
nonstop music in the incidental
bits and pieces of the world going by,
the exuberant excess of it all.

Room with Three Windows

Today when I sat in my study
and every word seemed used up,
I tried to imagine myself
as the room without me in it.

The three windows were all
equally ready to receive
sun and shade. When morning
arrived at the eastern one,
lightening the dark green leaves
on the lilac just outside,
the south-facing windows felt
for the sun even before it
turned the corner of the house.

I came close to being
as transparent as the windows
as I listened to maple leaves
in the wind, a catbird that likes
to sit in the lilac's shadows,
and a phoebe in the sun.

Catbird, lilac, shade, phoebe, sun,
even the rug's green-gold vines
coming alive in late afternoon sun,
all meant exactly the same thing.

And I saw clearly I could not be
the light that knew nothing of itself,

or the windows passing the light
from outside in, and I gave thanks,
returning to my desk in a room
continuing to make something
out of what is always here.

Last Things

I am always thinking about death—
my own mostly, but this morning

Augustine's, he who asked to be left alone
at the end, his only company

the six large-lettered penitential psalms
he tacked to his cell walls, a map

even a saint needs, I guess, on the journey
toward death the self keeps trying

to prepare itself for. So often I have prayed,
Teach me the way I should go, and *O Lord,*

heal me, for my bones are shaking with terror,
as if, in the repetition of those words,

each larval stage of my life might be let go.
But just as often I have been distracted

by dust on the windowsill dimpling with rain
or the yellow shine of afternoon sun

on the grass, by the rush and babble
of voices talking all at once in the next room,

or even a dog's barking—as Augustine
may have been, looking up now and again

from his prayer, arrested by an ordinary cloud
passing across the face of the sun

and the new shadows pooling on the floor,
the next thing still happening, still arriving

and being replaced, still restless, all of it
part of a world so hard to finish loving.

Luna Moths

The first time I woke up crying
from a puddle of sleep and found it

fluttering against a wall
like a dying leaf of spring green light.

The second I found lying lightly
on the ground, newly dead.

I brought it inside, and placed it
on a blank piece of paper

for my study. Palest green wings.
A thin red border, like a child's outline,

on the edges of its forewings
and hindwings. A yellow inner border

on its long, tailed hindwings.
Four white eyespots, ringed in yellow

and maroon. On that white
sheet of paper, it appeared to be

some beautiful, lost metaphor
of an indecipherable language.

I'd read the facts—the one week life span,
the way, because they do not eat,

the adults have no need of a mouth—by the time
I found the third, late at night

high on the wall of my kitchen.
I'd had too much to drink. I spoke to it

as if it were my own Buddhist teacher
here to teach me non-attachment,

the illusions of hunger, sex, rampant need.
I sat with it until the sun rose, toasting

its quick beauty, then the restfulness I found
in its body, and then those bright-eyed,

translucent green wings that seemed
to breathe more and more slowly before going

motionless. When I lifted it in my hand
I knew just how little the space was

between myself and nothingness.

Gift

How long can one man's lifetime last?
—Wang Wei

Long enough, he said to our tears,
to know *all of it is a gift.* We wanted
to hold him back from the dying

he was busy doing, nine months of working
his way through the Book of Subtractions:
first the relished taste of food and wine,

and then Yeats, the *Four Quartets,*
and the Psalms he could no longer read
alone. In the end, even the music

his children loaded on an I-Pod—
Mozart and Brahms to counter the morphine
that countered the bladed pains

that ran through his back—
became too difficult to listen to.
And yet he called each painful day a gift,

and held fiercely to each moment,
whatever it brought: swallows freelancing
in the wind, the odor of lilac

after a night's rain, the way sunlight settled
over the rug like a large dog—
nothing he earned, but accepted,

as he accepted the near identical looks
his children and his wife exchanged
when they saw how, daily, his cancer grew

towards the dread of his utter absence.
To all of it he said *yes.*
Yes to the pollen greening the roofs

of parked cars as his body withered,
and to the cold of the window glass
he leaned his cheek against,

and *yes,* to the nearly unendurable love
he felt for his wife and children
whose longing for him he could not

lessen, and to everything that remained
unsayable between them. And *yes,*
finally, to whatever came next, after

this life he had been given, this death.

Notes and Dedications

Dangling: the story of the monk told here is from Christopher Merrill's book, *Things of the Hidden God, Journey to the Holy Mountain*. The poem is dedicated to him.

Czeslaw Milosz's Glasses: this poem is dedicated to Gray Jacobik.

The Chair: this poem is dedicated to my late friend and colleague, John Wilson.

Erasure: this poem is dedicated to Andrew Von Hendy.

Walking with Ruskin: this poem is dedicated to Jack McCarthy.

Gift: this poem, too, is in honor of my friend, John Wilson.

CavanKerry's Mission

Through publishing and programming, CavanKerry Press
connects communities of writers with communities of readers.
We publish poetry that reaches from the page to include the
reader, by the finest new and established contemporary writers.
Our programming brings our books and our poets to people
where they live, cultivating new audiences and nourishing
established ones.

Other Books in
the Notable Voices Series

———

CavanKerry now uses only recycled paper in its book production. Printing this book on 30% PCW and FSC certified paper saved 2 trees, 1 million BTUs of energy, 127 lbs. of CO_2, 67 lbs. of solid waste, and 524 gallons of water.